D1809251

Joe

First published 1988 by Walker Books Ltd
Walker House, 87 Vauxhall Walk
London SE11 5HJ

Text © 1988 Bamber Gascoigne
Illustrations © 1988 Joe Wright

First printed 1988
Printed and bound by L.E.G.O., Vicenza, Italy

British Library Cataloguing in Publication Data
Gascoigne, Bamber
Amazing facts.
1. Curiosities and wonders – Juvenile literature
I. Title   II. Wright, Joe 1947-
032'.02   AG243

ISBN 0-7445-0747-2

The publishers are grateful for permission to use the following facts: first public lavatory, roller skater, tinned foods and Queen Elizabeth I's bath routine from *The Shell Book of Firsts* by Patrick Robertson (Michael Joseph and Ebury Press Ltd); first traffic light from *Eureka* by Edward de Bono (Thames and Hudson Ltd); the longest coma, woman swallowing objects, longest fall without a parachute and longest survival without food and water from *The Guinness Book of Records* (© Guinness Superlatives Ltd).

BAMBER GASCOIGNE'S
book of
AMAZING FACTS
illustrated by
JOE WRIGHT

WALKER BOOKS
LONDON

By the time Mozart was ten years old he had given numerous public performances on both the violin and the harpsichord in Austria, Germany, France, Belgium and England and had composed four violin sonatas, two symphonies and more than twenty other works.

The Spanish dramatist Lope de Vega (1562-1635) is believed to have written more than 2,200 plays, of which 468 survive. If the full number is correct, that means he wrote a new play every ten days throughout his working life. He also, to while away his spare time, composed 1,587 sonnets.

7

Swifts live almost their entire lives in the air. They feed by flying around at high speed with their large mouths wide open, literally drinking up the insects (they fly about 500 miles a day doing this). They wash and even mate on the wing. Indeed they only come to earth for the nesting season, which means that they spend nine months of the year in continuous flight. And coming down to earth means, for them, just clinging to vertical surfaces. If a swift lands on the ground, its feet are so small and weak that it will often not be able to launch itself into the air again and so will die.

OOOOOOH LOVELY!

Certain birds, such as starlings and jackdaws, like few things better than the sensation of ants crawling all over them. They will go and sit on an ant hill, rustling their feathers until the outraged insects are swarming on every part of the bird's skin. There is a practical reason. The ants, in their anger, give off formic acid, which is sufficiently poisonous to kill the fleas and other small parasites living on the bird.

Imagine that you couldn't get out of a pair of jeans that were becoming too tight for you until you had grown so much that the pressure inside, from your growth alone, split them open. Sounds a bit alarming. Yet that is what happens to a lobster every time it gets bigger. It splits its hard shell open, just from the pressure of the soft body growing inside. Then the unprotected creature crawls out of the crack and hides somewhere safe until its new and larger shell has hardened. And unlike you, the lobster goes on growing all its life. Thank your lucky stars!

In South America there are spiders with a leg span of up to ten inches. Not nice in the bath. At that size insects are no longer of much interest to them. Birds are what they fancy.

On 5 April 1795 the Prince of Wales, who would later be King George IV, had a nasty shock. "Harris," he said to his gentleman-in-waiting, "I am not well. Pray get me a glass of brandy." What had upset the Prince? He had just set eyes on his future wife, Princess Caroline of Brunswick, with whom a royal marriage had been arranged.

Royal princes used to have substitutes known as whipping boys, because it was considered improper to chastise the prince himself. When the prince did anything wrong, the other boy was whipped. If the whipping boy was a friend of the prince, the system did perhaps improve the royal behaviour a little. And no doubt the whipped friend could expect some special favours in later life when the prince became king.

A French family living north of Paris always took their cat with them on their summer holiday and always went to the same rented house near the Mediterranean, some 400 miles to the south. In 1982, just before Christmas, the cat went missing from the family home. They assumed she had been run over. But when they arrived for their holiday the next summer, there she was, waiting for them in the sun. The neighbours, who had recognized her and fed her, said she had arrived just before the New Year. So she had taken only a week to find her way on the 400-mile journey. She couldn't understand why a sensible family, with a dreary home in a suburb of Paris and a fine one near the Mediterranean, should choose to spend nearly all year in the suburbs.

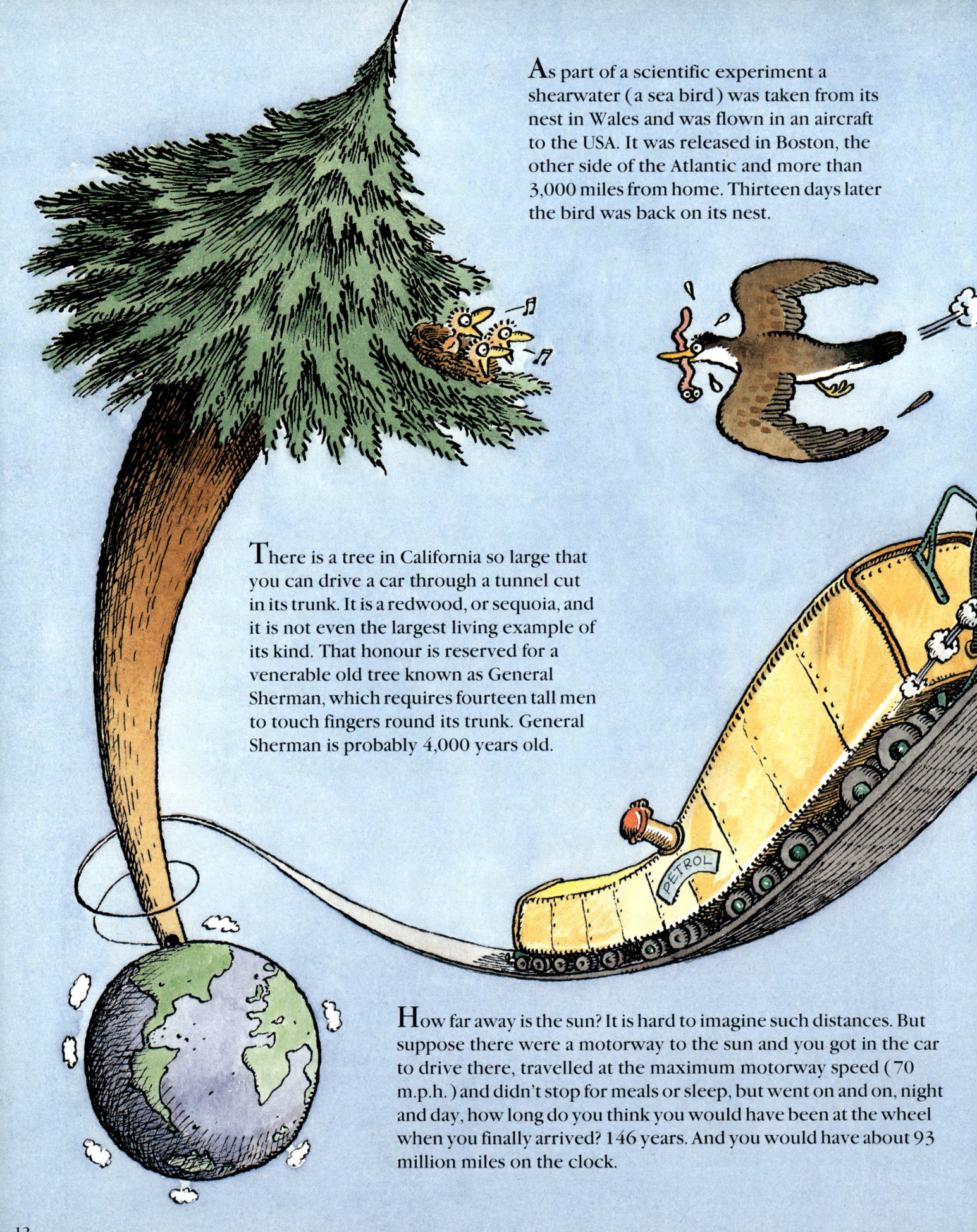

As part of a scientific experiment a shearwater (a sea bird) was taken from its nest in Wales and was flown in an aircraft to the USA. It was released in Boston, the other side of the Atlantic and more than 3,000 miles from home. Thirteen days later the bird was back on its nest.

There is a tree in California so large that you can drive a car through a tunnel cut in its trunk. It is a redwood, or sequoia, and it is not even the largest living example of its kind. That honour is reserved for a venerable old tree known as General Sherman, which requires fourteen tall men to touch fingers round its trunk. General Sherman is probably 4,000 years old.

How far away is the sun? It is hard to imagine such distances. But suppose there were a motorway to the sun and you got in the car to drive there, travelled at the maximum motorway speed (70 m.p.h.) and didn't stop for meals or sleep, but went on and on, night and day, how long do you think you would have been at the wheel when you finally arrived? 146 years. And you would have about 93 million miles on the clock.

By 1895 motor cars were easily capable of driving at 20 m.p.h. (about the speed of an Olympic athlete running 100 metres today) but this burst of speed was not much use to the eager motorist in Britain. A law, known as the Red Flag Act, specified that whenever a car was driven on a public road somebody should walk in front of it waving a red flag to warn passers-by of the approach of a dangerous vehicle.

The world's first traffic light was set up outside the Houses of Parliament in London in 1868 to cope with the regular traffic jam of horses and carriages. It seemed to work well until it blew up (the red and green lights were lit by gas), killing a policeman. It was almost fifty years before there was another traffic light.

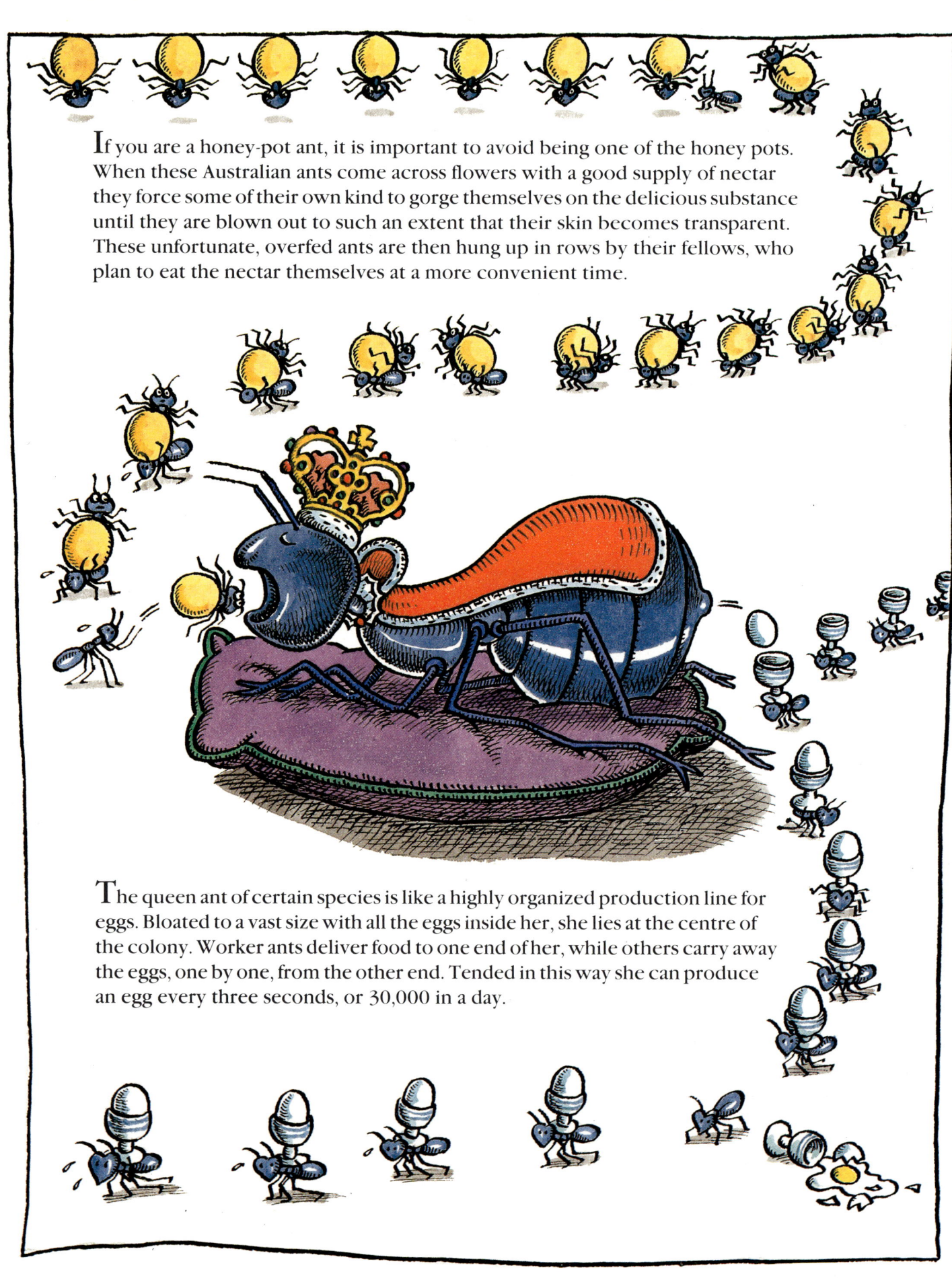

If you are a honey-pot ant, it is important to avoid being one of the honey pots. When these Australian ants come across flowers with a good supply of nectar they force some of their own kind to gorge themselves on the delicious substance until they are blown out to such an extent that their skin becomes transparent. These unfortunate, overfed ants are then hung up in rows by their fellows, who plan to eat the nectar themselves at a more convenient time.

The queen ant of certain species is like a highly organized production line for eggs. Bloated to a vast size with all the eggs inside her, she lies at the centre of the colony. Worker ants deliver food to one end of her, while others carry away the eggs, one by one, from the other end. Tended in this way she can produce an egg every three seconds, or 30,000 in a day.

The adult kangaroo stands almost six feet tall, but when a baby kangaroo (known as a joey) is born, it is just a little more than one inch long. And the very first thing this tiny joey has to do is climb up the fur of its huge mother's stomach – for us it would be like climbing up the outside of a fur-covered building many storeys high. When the journey is complete, the joey finds its way into the kangaroo's pouch, where a welcoming nipple and a much needed drink of milk awaits it. After that first experience the joey doesn't fancy looking out of the pouch for several weeks, but eventually it does begin to make journeys into the outside world.

Every second of the day and night, all round the year, four babies come into the world, which means that during the time it takes you to read this sentence aloud (assuming you are a fast reader) enough people will have been born to fill a double-decker bus and several of them would not even be able to find a seat.

A woman of forty-two was taken into hospital in Canada in 1927 with a pain in her stomach. The pain was not surprising. The surgeons found inside her 2,533 separate objects that she had swallowed, including 947 bent pins.

CONGRATULATIONS, MADAM. YOU HAVE GIVEN BIRTH TO 947 BENT PINS.

A very strange thing was discovered, in recent years, about the eggs of tortoises and many other reptiles. If you hatch a tortoise's egg at 82°F/28°C you get a gentleman tortoise, but if you hatch the same egg at 86°F/30°C you get a lady tortoise. Clearly the balance of the sexes depends on very reliable weather.

Archaeologists in Denmark dug up an almost perfectly preserved body in a peat bog. They announced that the man had died a very long time ago and had been preserved by the tannic acid in the water. The local people fell about laughing because they all recognized the corpse as old Red Sven, a local tramp who had recently vanished and who must have fallen into the bog when drunk. The newspapers made much of the foolishness of experts. Then the scientific reports came back from the laboratory. The body was about 1,600 years old!

Several such people have been found, all looking alarmingly lifelike. One was dug up in England in 1984, in a Cheshire peat marsh. He is known now as Pete Marsh and after a little patching up has moved to more comfortable lodgings in the British Museum.

Many rulers in the past, in ancient China for example, believed that they would need the spirits of their servants and of their horses to assist them in the next world. So dozens of people and animals were killed after a ruler's death and were buried with him in his tomb. But gradually people argued that clay statues of the horses and servants would be just as effective in the spirit world and it became the custom to place these in the tomb instead of sacrificed bodies. Certainly an example of human progress.

What is the dust in your bedroom made of? Where on earth does it come from? The answer is you. Most of it is tiny bits of your skin. As the top layer dries, it floats away in tiny particles to settle on a chest of drawers or picture frame. But this doesn't mean that you will soon be short of one layer of skin. New layers grow inside and gradually move outwards. The outer layer of your skin is completely replaced about every five days.

In the nineteenth century some people were so prim that they didn't like to mention the word trousers. So what did they say if they had to go out and buy this harmless and necessary garment? They asked, naturally, for a pair of "unmentionables".

I TOLD DICKY NOT TO EAT THOSE WORMS THE SCIENTISTS HAD THROWN OUT.

As part of an experiment, scientists taught a worm to move through a simple maze towards a light. They then chopped up the educated worm and fed it to another worm, and they found that this second worm moved correctly through the maze without having been taught to do so. They had proved that this particular learning process in the worm had involved a chemical change and so what had been learnt could be passed on with the chemicals themselves. Don't worry! There is no danger of pre-examination cannibalism in the classroom. There is no evidence at all that this will work with mathematics or French.

When the first escalator was installed on the London Underground (at Earl's Court in 1911), the authorities felt that passengers might consider the contraption alarming and difficult to use. They had a clever solution. They hired a one-legged man, known to his friends as Bumper Harris, and told him to ride up and down the escalator all the first day, showing how easy it was even for him. He was so successful that soon passengers were leaving their train at Earl's Court, riding happily on the escalator until the next train came in, and then continuing their journey. The *Illustrated London News* commented: "The device will, no doubt, be adopted elsewhere should its popularity continue."

It was impossible for buildings to be more than five or six storeys high until someone had invented a lift which the passengers could trust. That man was Elisha Otis and he demonstrated the safety of his lift in 1854 in a dramatic fashion at the Crystal Palace in New York. He was hauled high off the ground on a platform suspended from a rope. To the alarm of the spectators he then ordered an assistant to slash through the rope with an axe. Mr Otis remained, as he knew he would, safely aloft. His invention was a ratchet in the mechanism which was activated if the rope or cable broke.

The Falabella horses of Argentina have been bred to become smaller and smaller and are now the size of large dogs, varying in height from a Great Dane down to not much larger than a spaniel.

BRONCO BRAND MATCHES

The distance from the USSR to the USA is only fifty-three miles. Why? Because the Soviet Union stretches all the way east to the coast of Siberia in the northern Pacific and the United States stretches all the way west to the coast of Alaska in the northern Pacific. Between Siberia and Alaska is the Bering Strait, which at its narrowest point is fifty-three miles wide.

Food was first sealed in tins in about 1810, but it was another fifty years before the tin opener was invented. During those fifty years the cans were made of solid iron with a coating of tin inside. Each weighed about 1lb when empty and each carried a label saying "Cut round on top with a chisel and hammer".

Even so, many of these heavyweight tins were used. When William Parry went on an expedition to the Arctic in 1824, he took with him 12,000 lb of tinned carrots, together with many other foods. One of his tins of carrots and one of roast veal were brought back to England and were not opened until 1936. The 112-year-old veal was fed to a cat, which appeared to enjoy it and suffered no ill effects.

When Captain Matthew Webb had swum across the English Channel in 21 hours 43 minutes (from Dover to Calais in 1875), the Mayor of Dover publicly congratulated the hero and said he was certain nobody would ever again match this astonishing feat of endurance. The hundreds of swimmers who have done so since then include two British twelve-year-olds, Marcus Hooper (14 hours 37 minutes) and Samantha Druce (15 hours 27 minutes). And the Mayor of Dover might be surprised to hear of Michael Read, who by July 1984 had swum the Channel thirty times, and of Penny Dean who holds the fastest time of all for either sex, with a mere 7 hours 40 minutes.

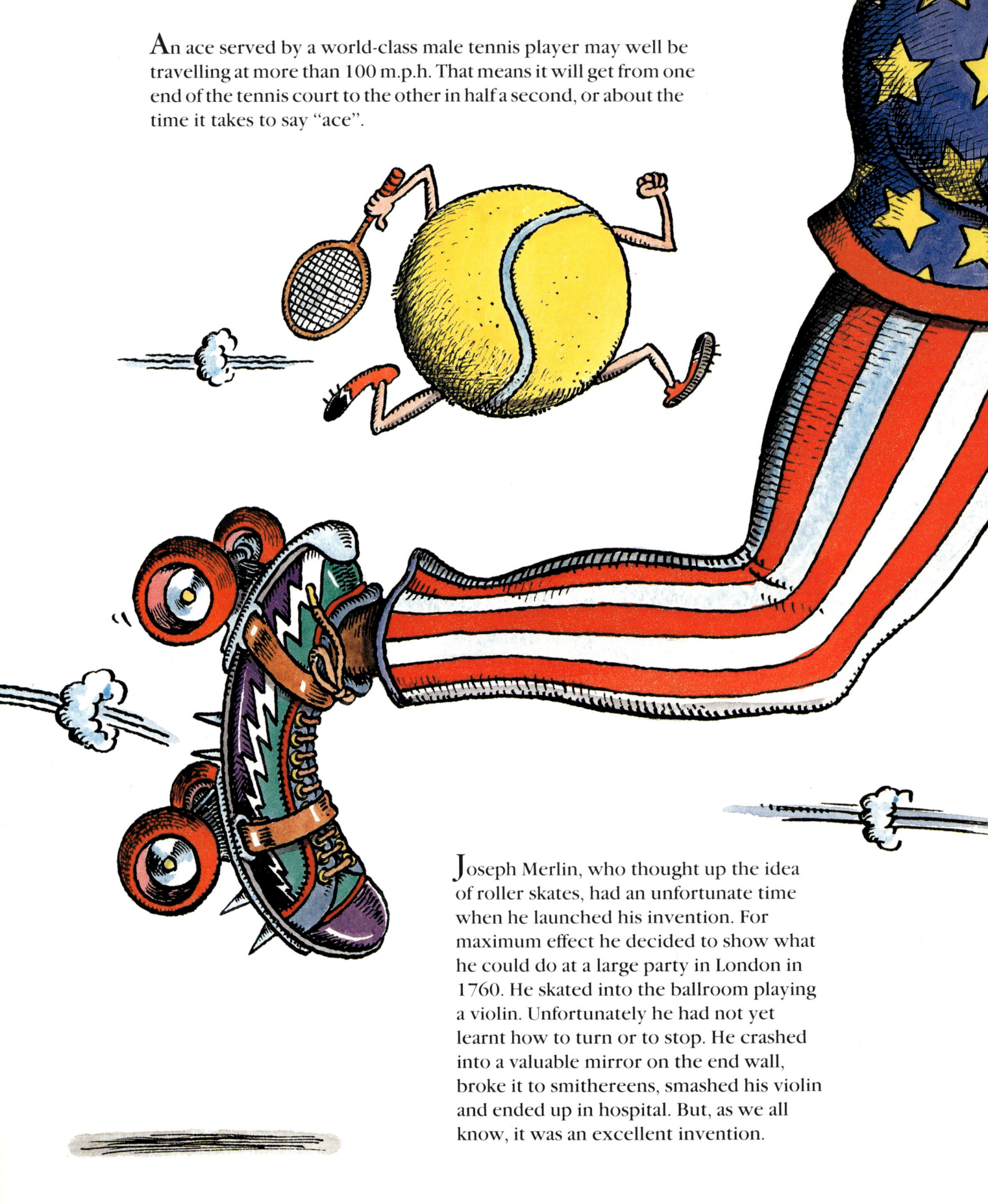

An ace served by a world-class male tennis player may well be travelling at more than 100 m.p.h. That means it will get from one end of the tennis court to the other in half a second, or about the time it takes to say "ace".

Joseph Merlin, who thought up the idea of roller skates, had an unfortunate time when he launched his invention. For maximum effect he decided to show what he could do at a large party in London in 1760. He skated into the ballroom playing a violin. Unfortunately he had not yet learnt how to turn or to stop. He crashed into a valuable mirror on the end wall, broke it to smithereens, smashed his violin and ended up in hospital. But, as we all know, it was an excellent invention.

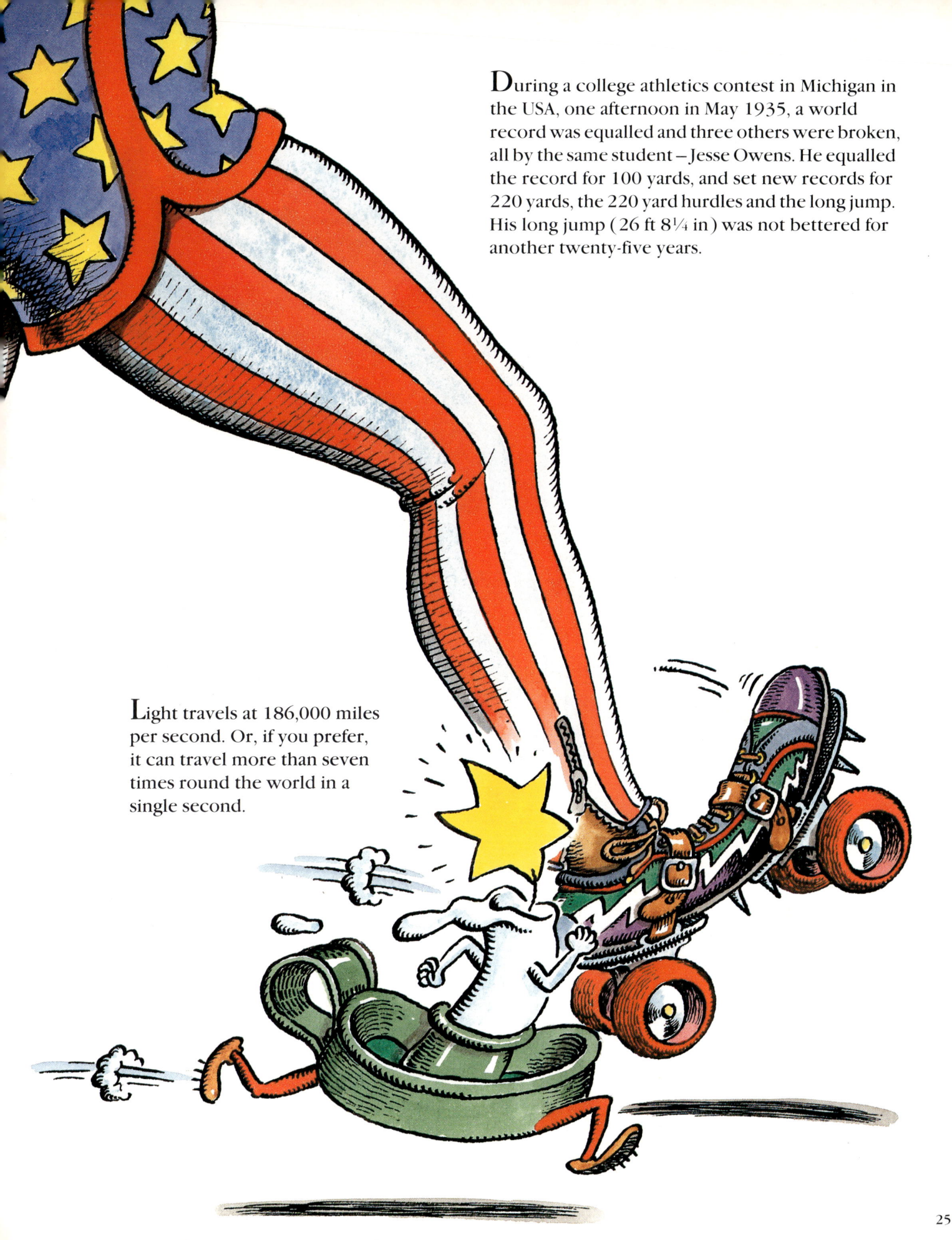

During a college athletics contest in Michigan in the USA, one afternoon in May 1935, a world record was equalled and three others were broken, all by the same student – Jesse Owens. He equalled the record for 100 yards, and set new records for 220 yards, the 220 yard hurdles and the long jump. His long jump (26 ft 8¼ in) was not bettered for another twenty-five years.

Light travels at 186,000 miles per second. Or, if you prefer, it can travel more than seven times round the world in a single second.

If all the arteries, veins and capillaries (the tiniest blood-carrying vessels) in your body were laid end to end, they would more than stretch round the entire world.

Consider the difficulties nature has placed in the way of the human parasites called blood flukes, tiny worms which cause unpleasant diseases such as bilharzia. The female worm must lay her eggs inside a human vein. The eggs must then pass out of the human being, through bladder or bowel, and reach fresh water before they hatch. There the young must find a snail and attach themselves to it while they grow. Later they must swim off in search of another human being. They must find a crack in the human skin (under a toenail being a favourite means of entry). Then they work their way into the person's body to find a vein in which to lay eggs and so restart the cycle. In spite of these obstacles the blood fluke thrives. Diseases caused by it are a common and serious problem.

Sea slugs are soft defenceless creatures with harmless waving tentacles on their backs. But some varieties have discovered that they can eat jellyfish that have stinging tentacles and the stinging part of the jellyfish, instead of being digested, makes its way from the sea slug's stomach to the end of its own tentacles. The sea slug is then as well armed as the jellyfish was, and with the identical weapon.

Have you ever looked closely at a flatfish, such as a plaice or flounder or sole, with its two eyes on the same side of the head? One eye looks a bit awkward and squashed, which is not exactly surprising. When such a creature is small, it has an eye on each side of its head and swims around upright in the sea, like any other fish. But one of the eyes gradually moves round, turns the corner and ends up on the other side, so that the adult fish can indulge in its habit of lying flat on the bottom, looking upwards (just) with both eyes.

All the stars you see in the sky are part of our galaxy, which is estimated to contain about 100,000 million stars, each of them much the same as our sun. And beyond all that, out of sight except to the most powerful telescopes, are thousands of millions of other galaxies, each of them much larger than everything that we can see in the heavens all bundled into one. The trouble with facts about the universe is that they are so amazing it is almost impossible to be amazed.

Until the age of space travel nobody had ever seen the back of the moon. Why not? Because the moon always shows us the same half, by turning one complete revolution on its own axis every time it circles the earth. It's like a ball on the end of a piece of string, swung round your head. You would only see one side of that until you stopped swinging it. And so far, fortunately, the moon swings on.

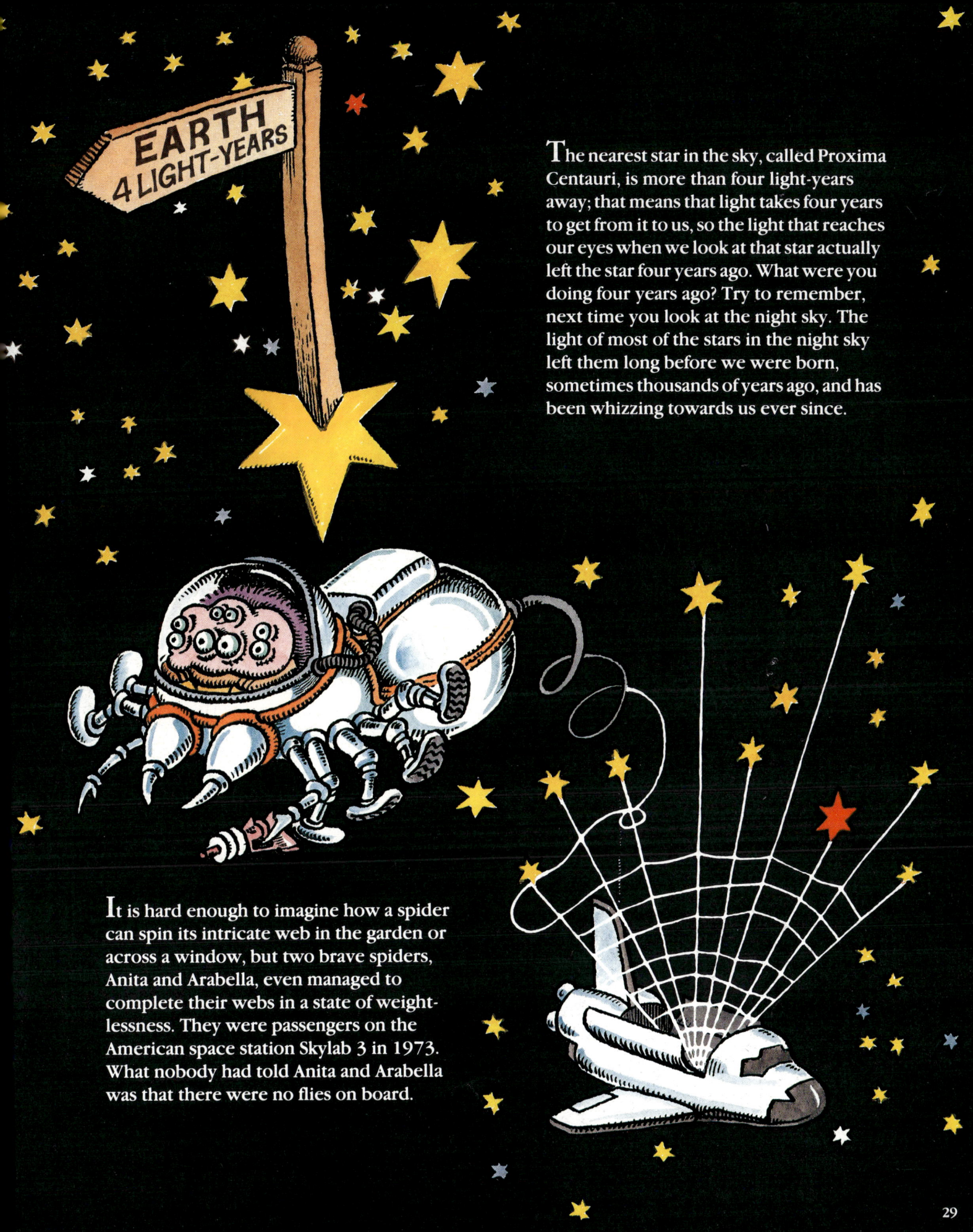

EARTH
4 LIGHT-YEARS

The nearest star in the sky, called Proxima Centauri, is more than four light-years away; that means that light takes four years to get from it to us, so the light that reaches our eyes when we look at that star actually left the star four years ago. What were you doing four years ago? Try to remember, next time you look at the night sky. The light of most of the stars in the night sky left them long before we were born, sometimes thousands of years ago, and has been whizzing towards us ever since.

It is hard enough to imagine how a spider can spin its intricate web in the garden or across a window, but two brave spiders, Anita and Arabella, even managed to complete their webs in a state of weightlessness. They were passengers on the American space station Skylab 3 in 1973. What nobody had told Anita and Arabella was that there were no flies on board.

The longest of the dinosaurs, diplodocus, was nearly ninety feet long. That is as long as seven fully grown elephants standing head to tail.

Bacteria are among the tiniest of living creatures and they are all over you. All over ME? you say with a shudder. All over everything, though all over some parts more than others. Under a human armpit, for example, on an area no larger than the head of a drawing pin, there will usually be about a million bacteria. That's the population of a city the size of Birmingham. And that's only a fraction of the available space. A whole armpit will yield up more than the populations of London, New York and Tokyo rolled into one. As an old saying goes, there's an awful lot going on in every nook of Granny.

The 21-year-old Guglielmo Marconi, inventor of radio, arrived in England in 1896 accompanied by his mother, to try to interest the British government in his brilliant device. He had an initial setback when the British customs officers smashed the machine, suspecting it was a dangerous object and its owner an Italian revolutionary. But that summer, after the necessary repairs, Marconi astonished the doubters by transmitting messages almost nine miles across the Bristol Channel.

Several of the smaller bats feed only on insects, which they have to catch in the air. A single bat may need as many as 1,000 insects in one night and, being blind, it can't even see them. So how does it collect this difficult meal? By sending out tiny clicking sounds, so short and so rapid that when the bat hears the echoes bouncing back off a moving insect, it will know where that insect is; and will know so precisely that it can swerve to gobble it up in the dark and then fly straight on in pursuit of the next.

The shrike is also known as the butcherbird because it keeps a larder. If it has killed a small lizard or a mouse, but is not particularly hungry at that moment, it will hang its victim from a thorn, as if on a meat hook, for a later meal at its own convenience.

In the old days sugar came in great roughly shaped cakes and the grocer had to hack off bits with a hammer and chisel to sell to the customer. Then somebody thought of a way of forming sugar into neat lumps, of the kind you see in sugar bowls today. The grocers put away their chisels and Mr Henry Tate – the Englishman in question – became a millionaire (and in the end, Sir Henry as well).

ONE LUMP OR TWO?

If you had a soft-boiled ostrich egg for breakfast, you could drop your spoon into the yolk and lose sight of it entirely. The egg would stand about five inches high – and that's without the eggcup!

Joe

33

The bee hummingbird of Cuba, the smallest bird in the world, weighs less than 0.07 of an ounce. This means that five of them would add up to less than the weight allowed for the cheapest airmail letter and thirty could go for the price of an ordinary inland letter in Britain.

The only amazing thing about the Welsh village of

Llanfairpwllgwyngyllgogerych

is its name, which apparently means St Mary's Church in the hollow of the white hazel near the rapid whirlpool of Llandysilio of the red cave.

The arctic tern is the world's greatest traveller, going further than any other creature to avoid the winter. It spends the northern summer near the North Pole and then flies 11,000 miles south to spend the southern summer near the South Pole. At the price of 22,000 miles a year, it gets more sunshine than even the most determined of human tourists.

Anyone receiving a letter from British Guiana in 1856, with a one-cent stamp on it would have done well to keep the envelope and hand it down in the family. Only one example of that stamp has survived. When it was last auctioned in 1980, it sold for nearly a million dollars.

$999,999.99

wyrndrobwllllantysiliogogogoch

In 1973 a Yugoslav aeroplane exploded in midair. An air hostess, Vesna Vulovic, fell more than 33,000 feet to the ground without a parachute. She was in a coma for twenty-seven days and in hospital for sixteen months, but she survived.

Andreas Mihavecz must have thought it was bad enough to be a passenger in a car crash on 1 April 1979 in Austria. But there was worse to come. He was put into a room to recover after the crash but then he was forgotten. Unfortunately the door was locked. Eighteen days later Andreas was discovered, barely alive. Some April Fools' Day! His only consolation is a place in *The Guinness Book of Records* as the longest recorded survival without food or water.

HELP!

EAT UP YOUR DROPPINGS, THEY'RE GOOD FOR YOU!

If you could watch a rabbit in its burrow, you would often see it doing something decidedly odd – greedily eating up its own warm droppings as soon as it has deposited them. The reason is that it wants another chance to digest the grass it has eaten, which is too tough for all the goodness to be extracted in a single passage through the rabbit's stomach.

When the first gentlemen's public lavatory with full flushing facilities was opened in London's Fleet Street, in 1852, its existence was advertised in *The Times* three times a week and 50,000 handbills were distributed describing the convenience of this convenience. Even so, only fifty-eight gentlemen used it during the first month – two a day (precisely, because the month was February and the year was a leap year).

Sloth means idleness and it is no accident that the name is given to an animal which lives in the jungle trees of South America. The sloth sleeps eighteen hours a day, relieves itself only once a week and is quite untroubled by the weeds and caterpillars which live in its hair. You can hardly get more slothful.

AMAZING!

ZZZ

An average blue whale, the largest creature in the world, weighs about the same as a flock of 2,200 sheep.

NOT MUCH GRASS ON THIS ISLAND, LARRY!

If a living sponge is squashed through a fine sieve, turning it into a texture much like apple purée, the cells will gradually re-form on the other side in their proper positions and eventually the sponge will be complete again and will go about its business as if nothing had happened.

There is a mountain below the sea which rises almost as high from the sea bed as Everest does above sea level. Lying north of New Zealand, it is 28,500 feet high (with its peak still 1,200 feet below the surface) as opposed to 29,028 feet for Everest.

There are certain fishes in the ocean which are themselves accomplished fishers and so are known as angler fish. Their rod is a long thin spine from the dorsal fin which droops forward over the head, to a position in front of the fish's own mouth. The bait on the end of this rod is a coloured or faintly luminous bobble. This attracts the attention of other fish, which swim close to discover what it is, thus placing themselves conveniently in front of the angler's jaws.

39

After the execution of Mary Queen of Scots at Fotheringay Castle in 1587, the executioner held up her bleeding head to show the crowd. To everyone's horror the head fell to the ground, leaving in the executioner's hand a wig of long auburn hair. It was seen that the Queen's own hair had been short and quite grey, even though she was only forty-four.

Girls live on average about 25 years longer than elephants, about 60 years longer than cats, 73 years longer than mice and – the only really annoying thing about all this for some of us – about 6 years longer than boys. (The life expectation in Britain of women is about 76 years and of men about 70.)

Jeremy Bentham was a philosopher who argued that the highest purpose in life was to achieve the greatest happiness of the greatest number of people. His friends must have wondered whether he practised what he preached when they heard, in 1832, the details of his will. He had instructed that they should all assemble for his body to be dissected in their presence. The skeleton was then to be cleaned, reconstituted, dressed in Bentham's own clothes and placed in University College, London, for the edification of future generations. He sits there still, in a glass case.

An early word for slimming was "banting" which was the name of a grossly
fat English undertaker, William Banting, who lost more than three stone in
1862 by changing to a special slimmers' diet. It would hardly seem so to us.
William proudly described his self-denying daily intake as follows:

——— FOR BREAKFAST ———
I take four or five ounces of beef, mutton, kidneys, broiled fish,
bacon or cold meat of any kind except pork;
a large cup of tea (without milk), a little biscuit, or one ounce of dry toast.

——— FOR DINNER ———
Five or six ounces of any fish except salmon, any meat except pork,
any vegetable except potato, one ounce of dry toast,
fruit out of a pudding, any kind of poultry or game, and two or three glasses
of good claret, sherry, or Madeira – champagne, port and beer forbidden.

——— FOR TEA ———
Two or three ounces of fruit, a rusk or two, and a cup of tea without milk or sugar.

——— FOR SUPPER ———
Three or four ounces of meat or fish, similar to dinner, with a glass or two of claret.

——— FOR NIGHTCAP ———
If required, a tumbler of grog (gin, whisky, or brandy, without sugar)
or a glass or two of claret or sherry.

If there is a stink of rotting meat in the garden, it doesn't have to be a dead rat. There are some flowers which give off that smell to attract flies which will pollinate them, the way bees pollinate the sweeter-smelling flowers. Best not planted under the kitchen window!

One of the problems for a male penguin when it comes to choosing a mate is that it is almost impossible to tell, from appearances alone, whether another penguin is male or female. The bird's way of finding out is very practical. He intends to give a pebble to his loved one, as soon as he can locate her. So he picks up a pebble and lays it at the feet of any likely-looking penguin who is standing alone. If he gets a sharp peck and the offer of a fight, he knows he has made an improper advance to another male and so he moves on, taking the pebble. If he gets no reaction at all, the other bird is probably a female who is already paired. But if his pebble is received with a courteous bow, then he has found his own true love at last.

Everything arrives upside down in your head. The reason is that the light comes through a small hole in your eye (the black spot in the middle, the pupil) with the result shown in the picture.

So how do we avoid seeing the floor as the ceiling? Somehow the brain just decides to turn the picture upside down once more, to make it the right way up, and this was proved by an extraordinary experiment. Some people were given spectacles which had the effect of turning things upside down. So the people wearing these spectacles really did see other people's feet above their heads. But then, after a few days, something in their brains said "this is ridiculous". Their brains adjusted and suddenly, with the spectacles on, these people were seeing everything the right way up again.

The really alarming time was when they took the spectacles off, because then they found they were seeing everything upside down with their own eyes. Would their brains be able to do the trick of adjustment yet again, or were they stuck for life? You will be pleased to hear that the human brain triumphed over these fiendish tricks. Things were soon back to normal, indeed rather more quickly than before.

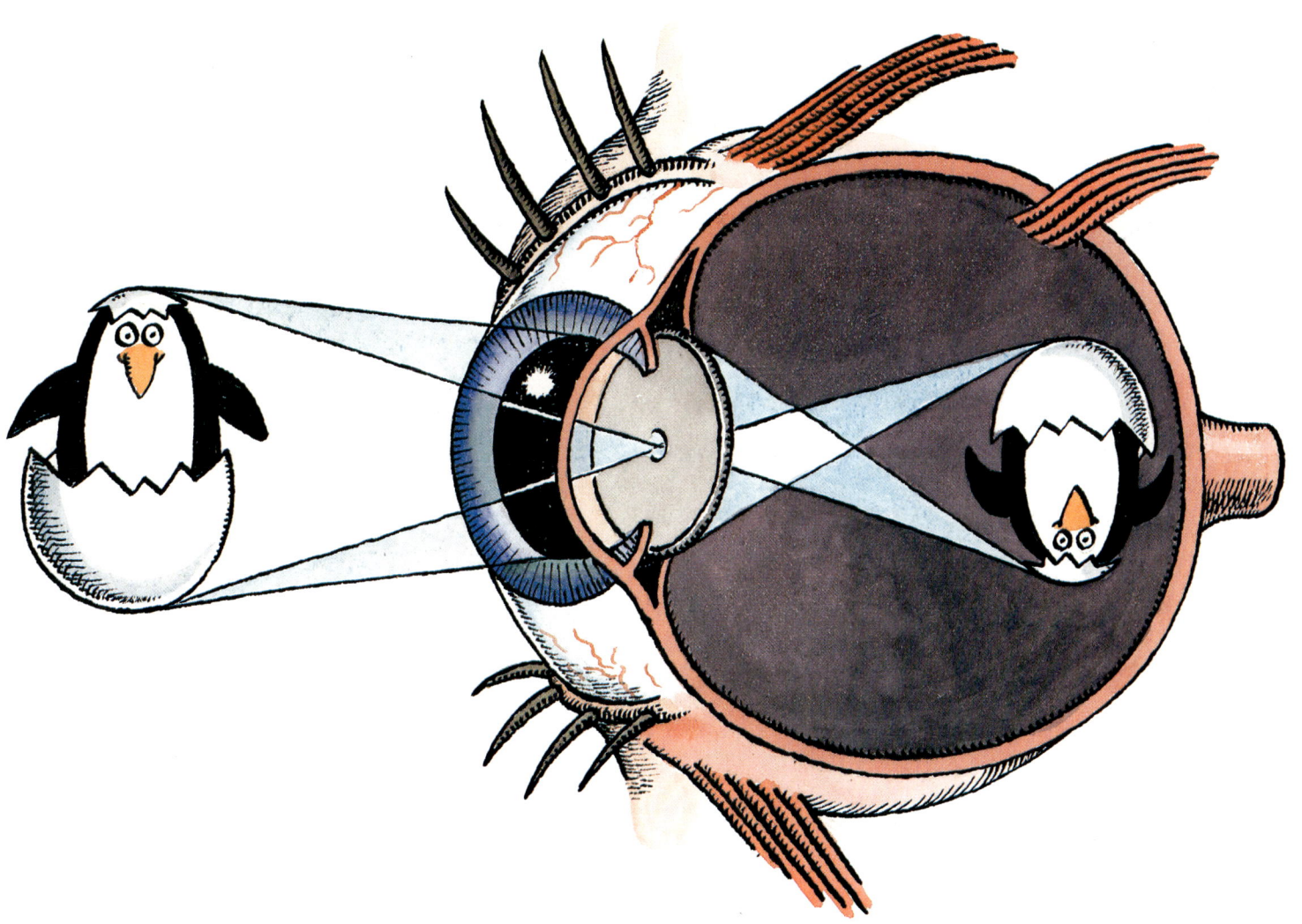

The first man to realize the possibility of deep-freezing food died as a result of his inspiration. Sir Francis Bacon was driving near Highgate in his carriage one wintry day in March 1626, when the idea struck him that a very cold temperature might prevent meat from rotting. He stopped the carriage, bought a chicken and set about stuffing it full of snow. In doing so he caught a chill from which he died three weeks later.

The worrying thing is that the sun will eventually burn itself out, bringing to an end life on earth. The not so worrying thing is that this is thought likely to happen in about 10,000 million years' time.

In 1721 Princess Caroline, who was then the Princess of Wales, decided that her two small daughters should be protected against smallpox by the newly discovered method of inoculation. But she had to be certain that there was no danger to the royal infants, so she arranged for an unusual offer to be made to six prisoners who were then in Newgate Gaol under sentence of death. If they would agree to be inoculated they would all be pardoned. So, if they survived the experiment, they would be free men and if not . . . Either way it would mean no more gaol. All six accepted. And all six lived to tell the tale in freedom. The little princesses survived too, and inoculation rapidly became the fashion.

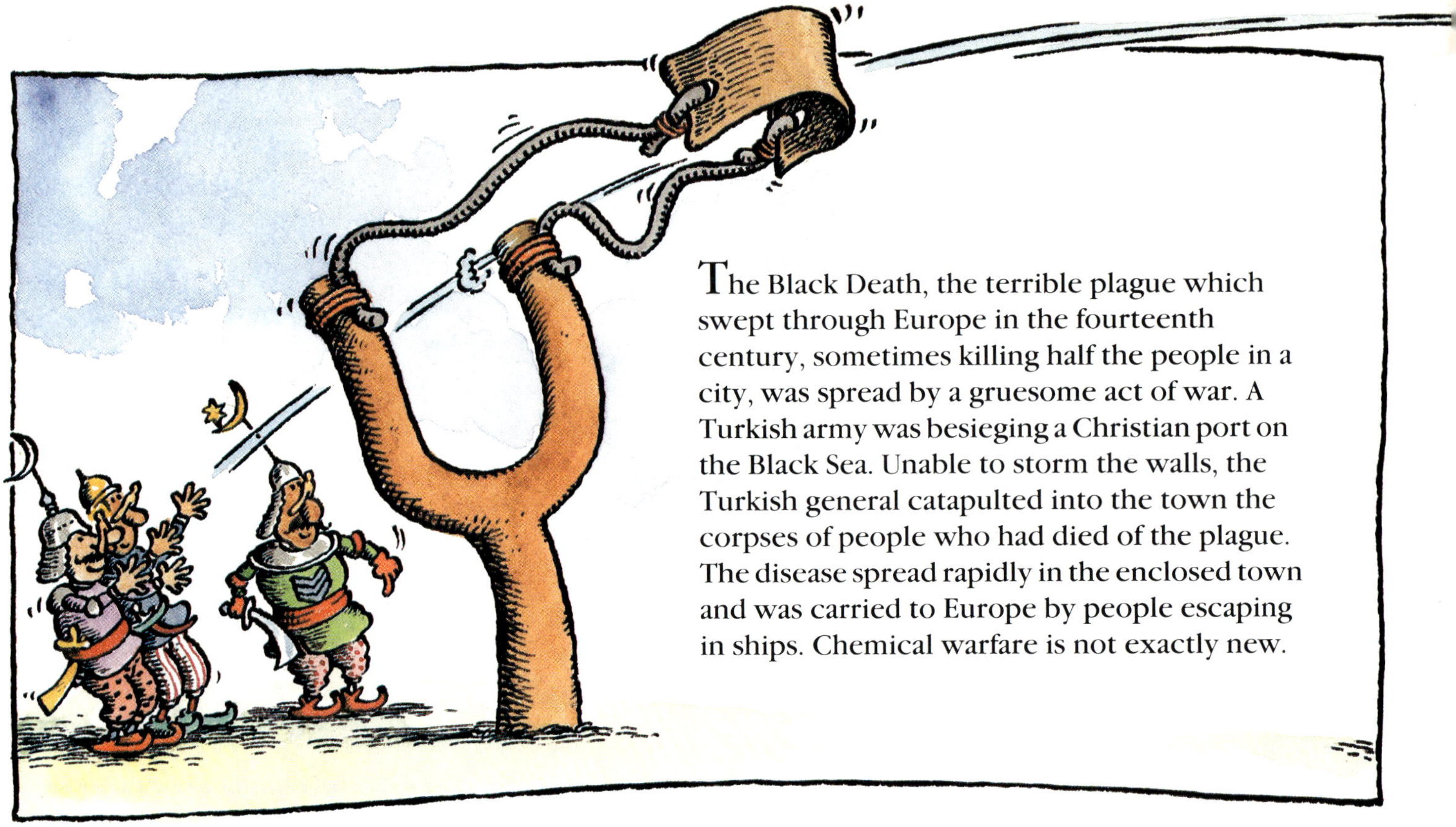

The Black Death, the terrible plague which swept through Europe in the fourteenth century, sometimes killing half the people in a city, was spread by a gruesome act of war. A Turkish army was besieging a Christian port on the Black Sea. Unable to storm the walls, the Turkish general catapulted into the town the corpses of people who had died of the plague. The disease spread rapidly in the enclosed town and was carried to Europe by people escaping in ships. Chemical warfare is not exactly new.

A French music hall artist, Joseph Pujol, known as Le Pétomane, made an unusual career for himself in the 1890s. He learnt how to break wind with a large range of different sounds. He could suck air into his intestine and then force it out again imitating a violin, or a trombone, or tearing fabric, or a gunshot. He certainly proved the saying – it's an ill wind that blows nobody any good.

If you live an average length of time you can expect to gobble up about 50 tons of food and drink 10,000 gallons of liquid.

Phineas T. Barnum, the greatest of all American showmen, made an unusual request when he was on his deathbed. He asked the editor of a New York paper to publish his obituary in advance, so that he would have the pleasure of reading it. (Obituaries, unlike reviews, can be relied on to be flattering, so why waste them?) The editor complied and Barnum died two weeks later. Another American who read his own obituary was the author Mark Twain, who was wrongly reported dead while travelling in Europe. He sent off an immediate cable: "The report of my death was an exaggeration."

THE REPORT OF MY DEATH WAS AN EXAGGERATION.

The earth we live on seems unimaginably old. It is believed to have come into existence about 4,500 million years ago – a great many years. Yet that is less than one year each for every man, woman and child alive on earth today – estimated now at about 4,700 million. You could just as well say that the earth we live on seems unimaginably crowded.

All the golden hamsters in captivity throughout the world are descended from a single couple captured in Syria in 1930. An average human couple, married in that same year, would now have grandchildren and perhaps some great-grandchildren, but they would be unlikely to have more than twenty descendants. But a hamster has about fifteen young every year. Each pair of young will soon themselves be having fifteen a year. At that rate the original Adam and Eve from Syria could, at a pinch, manage a million descendants in about seven years.

Mating is a dangerous business for male spiders because the females are hard to please and many will eat almost anything, including a lover. One type of male solves the problem by catching an insect, wrapping it up nicely in silk and offering it cautiously to his loved one. While she is busy unwrapping her present, he throws a few strands of silk over her, tying her to the ground just long enough for him to complete his courtship before he scuttles away to safety. Even so not all get away, sometimes giving the female two meals where she had been offered only one.

The deathwatch beetle often makes a loud clicking noise as it bores its way through the beams of old buildings. An ancient superstition said that the sound meant the approach of someone's death. In fact it is a mating call. The romantic insect, mad for love, makes the noise by banging its head against the wall.

CLICK CLICK CLICK CLICK CLICK

THEY'RE AT IT AGAIN!

51

Queen Elizabeth I was considered by her contemporaries to be exceptionally fastidious about her personal cleanliness. She took a bath once a month "whether she needed it or no".

The great French tightrope walker, Blondin, made a speciality of crossing the Niagara Falls in all sorts of different ways – wheeling a wheelbarrow, or on a bicycle, or with a stove on which he cooked an omelette. On one occasion, when he was carrying a man across on his shoulders, the passenger understandably fidgeted, nervous at the sight of the yawning space and torrent of water below. "I must ask you to sit still," said Blondin, "or I will have to put you down."

It is not known whether anybody gave a funny look at the Irish spinning maid Betty Burke, who was so eager to catch a boat to the island of Skye in June 1746. If they did you could hardly blame them, because young Betty was Bonnie Prince Charlie in disguise, trying to escape from English troops after the failure of his attempt to seize the crown. Betty got her boat and Charlie eventually made his way to safety in France.

In February 1764 the Bishop of Osnabrück was living in London instead of among his flock at Osnabrück in Germany. If you had been introduced to him you would have had to be unusually respectful because he was a prince of the British royal family, being the second son of George III. But what would have struck you more than anything else was the bishop's age. He was six months old. The bishopric was well paid. And his father, who was also ruler of that part of Germany, thought it would suit the boy.

William Pitt (1759-1806) became Chancellor of the Exchequer when he was twenty-three and Prime Minister when he was twenty-four. He remained Prime Minister until he was forty-one. This means that he left 10 Downing Street after nearly eighteen years in office, at a younger age than any Prime Minister since then has entered it.

One of the famous geysers in Yellowstone National Park in the USA has been aptly given the name of Old Faithful. Most of the time nothing seems to be happening, but at almost regular intervals – usually just a little more than an hour – Old Faithful suddenly erupts, sending a beautiful fountain of boiling water about 150 feet into the air (that's as high as a fifteen-storey building). In fact the old geyser has been known to delay as little as thirty-three and as much as ninety-three minutes between eruptions. But for the crowds always waiting to see it blow its top, a little uncertainty only adds to the excitement.

At Pompeii, in Italy, there can be seen the exact shapes of people killed as they ran or crawled away from the great eruption of Vesuvius in AD 79. Their shapes have been preserved because the volcanic dust settled around their fallen bodies and then solidified. With time their bodies crumbled away, leaving cavities in the rock. Scientists were later able to fill these cavities with plaster of Paris and so recapture the exact shapes of the fleeing victims.

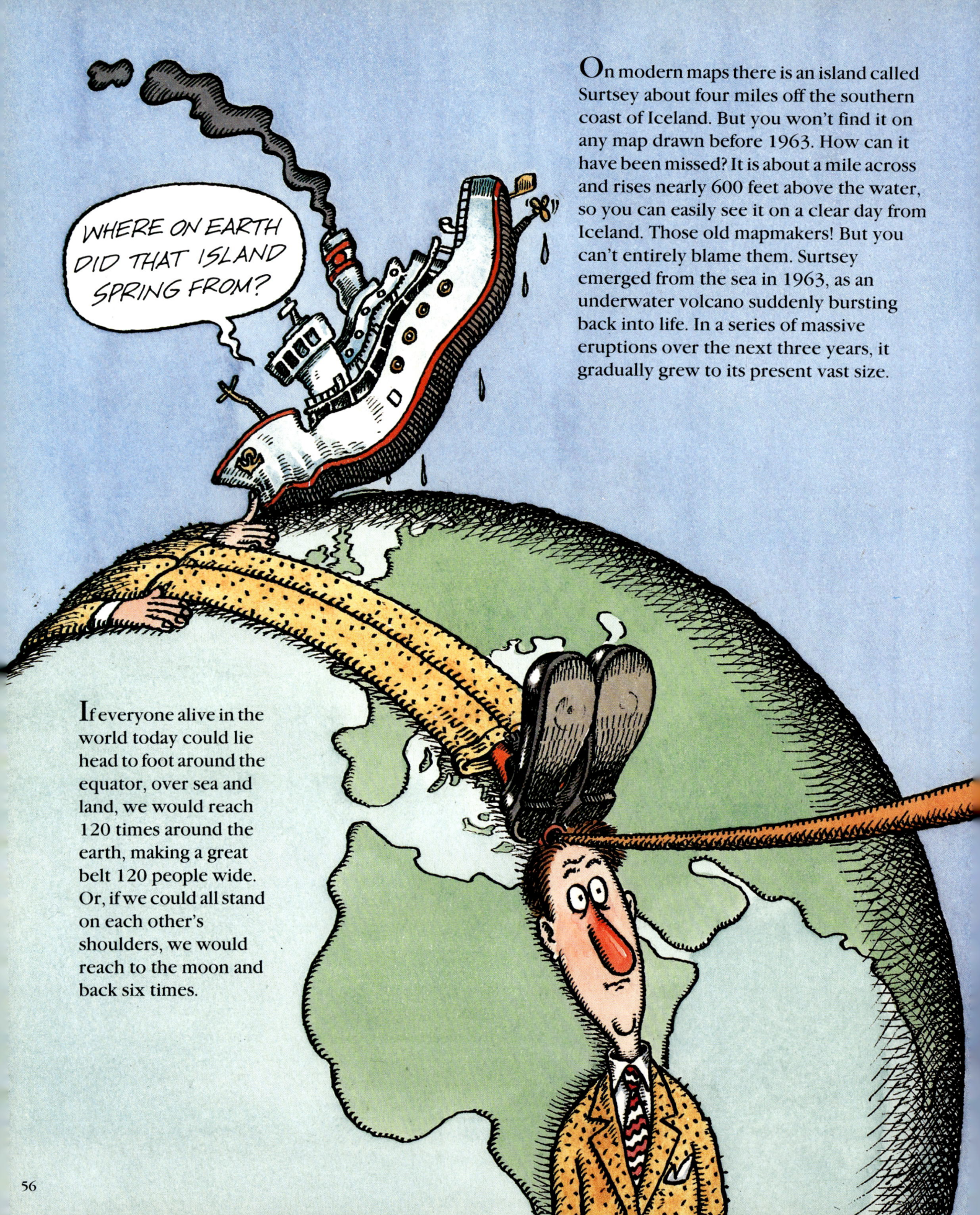

On modern maps there is an island called Surtsey about four miles off the southern coast of Iceland. But you won't find it on any map drawn before 1963. How can it have been missed? It is about a mile across and rises nearly 600 feet above the water, so you can easily see it on a clear day from Iceland. Those old mapmakers! But you can't entirely blame them. Surtsey emerged from the sea in 1963, as an underwater volcano suddenly bursting back into life. In a series of massive eruptions over the next three years, it gradually grew to its present vast size.

WHERE ON EARTH DID THAT ISLAND SPRING FROM?

If everyone alive in the world today could lie head to foot around the equator, over sea and land, we would reach 120 times around the earth, making a great belt 120 people wide. Or, if we could all stand on each other's shoulders, we would reach to the moon and back six times.

Saint Simeon Stylites was a monk, some 1,500 years ago in Syria, who so wanted peace and quiet for his prayers that he lived inside a circular wall in the middle of the desert. But he became famous as a holy man and crowds came out to visit him. To escape from them he built himself a pillar and lived on top of that. That made him even more famous and more crowds came. So he built still higher and spent the last twenty years of his life on top of a pillar fifty feet high, surrounded by an almost permanent crowd of admiring pilgrims. They would shout up their worries to him and he, being a holy man, would shout down his religious advice. It was the world's first agony column.

OUCH!

We all consist almost entirely of space. The reason is that the particles making up all matter are infinitely small compared with the gaps between them. So, if we could make a needle that was unimaginably thin, it could be pushed straight through you without touching any part of you. Indeed it could be pushed straight through the world, from Britain to Australia, without bumping into anything solid. We know this because there are tiny particles called neutrinos, which do just that. They arrive all the time from outer space, pass through us and then carry on through the earth and out the other side. And only one in many million neutrinos ever bumps into anything on the way through.

EEK!

The Aztec people, who ruled Mexico 500 years ago, had an unfortunate belief that a breakfast of human blood was essential for the sun if it were to be given the strength to get up each morning. So they arranged an endless succession of human sacrifices — usually of enemies captured in battle — to save the world from lapsing into eternal night. Because of their conviction that this theory was right, it was impossible for them to stop the sacrifices — and without stopping the sacrifices it was impossible for them to discover that the theory was wrong.

The human flea can live up to six months without a meal, but it does have to have a drop of blood before mating.

One of the problems with early false teeth was how to keep the top set in place. Some people even went so far as to hook them onto their gums. In the eighteenth century a French dentist, Pierre Fauchard, had a better idea. He joined the upper and lower rows of teeth at the back with a strong spring, forcing them apart. This kept the upper denture safely in place at the top. But it also meant that you had to work very hard, concentrating all the time, to close your mouth when you were wearing the contraption. Fauchard's patients spent much of their time looking as if they had heard a really amazing fact.

When Elaine Esposito died in 1978 in the USA, she was forty-three years old. Yet she had never known life at any age older than six. She was that age when she went into hospital to have her appendix out in 1941. After the operation she went into a coma, and remained in it for thirty-seven years — the longest coma in history.

INDEX

A

angler fish, behaviour 39
animal, largest 38-9
ant, behaviour 14
arctic tern, greatest traveller ... 34
arteries, length of human 26
athletic records 24-5
Aztec, human sacrifice 58

B

Bacon, Sir Francis 44
bacteria on human skin 31
Banting, William 41
Barnum, Phineas T. 48
bat, navigation 32
bee hummingbird, size 34
Bentham, Jeremy 40
bilharzia disease 26
bird: feeding habits 8, 32
        greatest traveller 34
        homing instinct 12
        parasites on 8
        smallest 34
Bishop of Osnabrück 54
Black Death 46
Blondin 52-3
blood fluke parasite 26
blood vessels, length of human .. 26
blue whale 38-9
Bonnie Prince Charlie 53
burial customs, Chinese 18
butcherbird's larder 32

C

capillaries, length of human ... 26
car, early 13
Caroline, Princess of Brunswick . 10
Caroline, Princess of Wales 45
cat, travelling 11
coma, longest 59
cross-channel swimming 23

D

Dean, Penny 23
death: Chinese 18
        comatose 59
        peat marsh 18
        wrongly reported 48
deathwatch beetle, mating call .. 51
dentures, fixing 59
dinosaur, longest 30-31
distance: earth to sun 12
        round earth 56
        US to USSR 22-3
Druce, Samantha 23
dust particles on human skin .. 19

E

earth: age 49
        distance from sun 12
        population 16, 49, 56
        size 56
eating habits: bat 32
                human 47
                rabbit 36
                sea slug 27
                shrike 32
eggs: ant production of 14
        ostrich, size of 33
        tortoise, sex determination
        of 17
Elizabeth I 52
escalator, first 20
Esposito, Elaine 59

F

Falabella horse 21
fall without parachute 35
false teeth, fixing 59
Fauchard, Pierre 59
flatfish, movement of eyes 27
flea, mating habits 58
flowers, smelly 42
food: bat 32
        frozen, first 44
        human intake 47
        rabbit 36
        sea slug 27
        shrike 32

G

galaxies in outer space 28
geyser, "Old Faithful" 55

H

hamster, origins 50
honey-pot ant, behaviour 14
Hooper, Marcus 23
horse, smallest 21
human sacrifice, Aztec 58
hummingbird, smallest 34

I

inoculation for smallpox 45

K

kangaroo birth 15

L

lavatory, first public 37
Le Pétomane 46
life span, human and animal ... 40
lift, first 21
light: falling on human eye 43
        speed 25
light-years 29
lobster, shedding shell 9

M

Marconi, Guglielmo 31
Mary, Queen of Scots 40
matter, particles of 57
Merlin, Joseph 24
Milhavecz, Andreas 36
moon, back of 28
mountain, undersea 38
Mozart, Wolfgang Amadeus 6

N

neutrinos, particles of matter .. 57
Niagra Falls, crossing 52-3

O

"Old Faithful" geyser 55
ostrich egg, size 33
Otis, Elisha 21
Owens, Jesse 24-5

P

parasites: bird 8
     human 26
Parry, William 22-3
peat marsh man 18
penguin, mating habits 42
pins, swallowed 17
Pitt, William 54
place name, Welsh 34-5
plague 46
Pompeii 55
population figures 16, 49, 56
Prince of Wales, later George IV . 10
Proxima Centauri, nearest star . 29
Pujol, Joseph 46

R

rabbit, eating habits 36
radio, invention 31
Read, Michael 23
records: animal, largest 38-9
    athletics 24-5
    bird, greatest traveller . . 34
    bird, smallest 34
    coma, longest 59
    cross-channel
     swimming 23
    dinosaur, longest . . 30-31
    egg, size 33
    escalator, first 20
    frozen food, first 44
    horse, smallest 21
    lavatory, first public . . 37
    lift, first 21
    mountain, undersea . . . 38
    radio, first 31
    roller skates, first 24
    smallpox inoculation,
     first 45
    speed 24-5
    stamp, most valuable . 35
    star, nearest 29
    survival without food or
     water, longest 36
    tin can, first 22-3
    traffic light, first 13
    tree, largest 12
Red Flag Act 13
redwood tree 12
roller skates, invention 24

S

sea slug, eating habits 27
sequoia, largest tree 12
shearwater, homing instinct . . . 12
shrike, eating habits 32
skin: bacteria on human 31
    dust from human 19
Skylab 3 29
slimming diet 41
sloth, behaviour 37
smallpox inoculation 45
space travel, spiders in 29
spider: leg span 9
    mating habits 51
    space travel 29
sponge, cell behaviour 38
stamp, most valuable 35
stars, distance and number . . . 28-9
Stylites, St Simeon 57
sugar lumps, origin 33
sun: burning out 44
    distance 12
    sacrifice to 58
Surtsey, eruption 56
survival: fall without parachute . . 35
    without food or water . . 36
swift, flight 8
swimming, cross-channel
    records 23

T

Tate, Sir Henry 33
tennis ball, speed 24
tin can, first 22-3
tombs, Chinese 18
tortoise, sex determination 17
traffic light, first 13
tree, largest 12
trousers ("unmentionables") . . 19
Twain, Mark 48

V

Vega, Lope de 7
veins, length of human 26
Vesuvius, eruption 55
vision, human 43
volcano, underwater eruption . 56
Vulovic, Vesna 35

W

Webb, Captain Matthew 23
Welsh place name 34-5
whale, blue 38-9
whipping boy, custom 10
worms, trained 20

Y

Yellowstone National Park 55